Lerner SPORTS

SPORTS VIPs

MEET CEEDEE LAMB

MARGARET J. GOLDSTEIN

Lerner Publications ◆ Minneapolis

Lerner Publications Company
An imprint of Lerner Publishing Group, Inc.
241 First Avenue North
Minneapolis, MN 55401 USA

For reading levels and more information, look up this title at www.lernerbooks.com.

Main body text set in Aptifer Slab LT Pro. Typeface provided by Linotype AG.

Editor: Anne E. Hill

Library of Congress Cataloging-in-Publication Data

Names: Goldstein, Margaret J. author.
Title: Meet CeeDee Lamb : Dallas Cowboys superstar / Margaret J. Goldstein.
Description: Minneapolis, MN : Lerner Publications, [2025] | Series: Lerner sports. Sports VIPs | Includes bibliographical references and index. | Audience: Ages 7–11 | Audience: Grades 2–3 | Summary: "Dallas Cowboys wide receiver CeeDee Lamb plays football with skill, speed, and plenty of style. Lamb grew up in Louisiana and moved to Texas after Hurricane Katrina in 2005. Explore his journey to NFL stardom"—Provided by publisher.
Identifiers: LCCN 2024019020 (print) | LCCN 2024019021 (ebook) | ISBN 9798765649244 (library binding) | ISBN 9798765662441 (paperback) | ISBN 9798765658475 (epub)
Subjects: LCSH: Lamb, CeeDee, 1999– | Football players—United States—Biography—Juvenile literature.
Classification: LCC GV939.L24 G65 2025 (print) | LCC GV939.L24 (ebook) | DDC 796.332092 [B]—dc23/eng/20240516

LC record available at https://lccn.loc.gov/2024019020
LC ebook record available at https://lccn.loc.gov/2024019021

Manufactured in the United States of America
1-1011064-53536-8/8/2024

TABLE OF CONTENTS

RECORD BREAKER

The Dallas Cowboys needed a big play. They were backed up near their end zone on third down. Quarterback Dak Prescott thought fast. He broke free from a tough Detroit Lions defense. Prescott threw the ball to Cowboys wide receiver CeeDee Lamb at the 50-yard line. Lamb ran into the end zone for a touchdown. Dallas fans went wild. It was a 92-yard touchdown!

The Cowboys won the game 20–19. It was an exciting win late in the 2023 season. But even more thrilling was Lamb's play that night. He caught 13 passes and had 227 receiving yards. This gave him a total of 122 receptions and 1,651 receiving yards. These were new Cowboys single-season records.

FAST FACTS

DATE OF BIRTH: April 8, 1999
POSITION: wide receiver
LEAGUE: National Football League (NFL)

PROFESSIONAL HIGHLIGHTS: was the 17th pick in the 2020 draft; set Dallas Cowboys single-season records for receptions and receiving yards; led the league in receptions in 2023

PERSONAL HIGHLIGHTS: attended the University of Oklahoma; has two dogs, Saint and Hendrix; works with the Boys & Girls Clubs of Greater Dallas

CeeDee Lamb (*right*) celebrates a touchdown with Cowboys quarterback Dak Prescott (*left*) in a game against the Detroit Lions.

In only his fourth season in the NFL, Lamb was making moves. Coaches, players, and reporters were amazed at how he caught the football. He could catch with one hand. He could even catch with his feet clinging to the back of the end zone.

Prescott said that Lamb would break many football records. "He's continuing to get better, wants to get better, and is hungry for the ball," Prescott said. "He's going to continue to stack these records each and every year. This is only the beginning."

Lamb races down the field in a game against the Green Bay Packers.

CHAPTER 1

FOOTBALL ROOTS

Cedarian DeLeon Lamb was born on April 8, 1999. He spent his early years in New Orleans, Louisiana's biggest city. He has two brothers and two sisters. His parents, Cliff Lamb and Leta Ramirez, divorced after Hurricane Katrina hit their city in 2005.

The hurricane flooded parts of the city. It forced the Lambs and other families to move. Cedarian's parents decided to live in separate homes in Houston, Texas.

Parts of New Orleans were flooded after Hurricane Katrina in 2005.

SUPER SPORTS SCOOP

CeeDee comes from a family of talented football players. His dad played football at MidAmerica Nazarene University in Kansas. His uncle Adam Lamb played at Texas Southern University. His uncle Chester Ramirez Jr. was on the US Air Force Academy football team.

Cedarian and his siblings continued to spend time with each of their parents. Cedarian loved watching football. He cheered hardest for the Louisiana State University Tigers. Cedarian started playing football as a young boy. One of his peewee coaches thought he needed a nickname. He shortened Cedarian to CeeDee.

CeeDee's uncle Adam Lamb (*left*) played football for Texas Southern University in 2000.

CeeDee was a standout at Foster High School in Richmond, Texas. "CeeDee was the best player I've ever been around," said his high school coach Shaun McDowell. During his senior year, CeeDee caught 98 passes. He had 2,023 receiving yards and scored 33 touchdowns. The team went 14–1 that year. College coaches took notice. CeeDee got many scholarship offers.

CHAPTER 2

FINDING THE END ZONE

In 2017, Lamb chose to attend the University of Oklahoma. He studied communications. On the football field, he had two positions: wide receiver and punt returner. He excelled at both.

Lamb's three years at Oklahoma were full of great receptions. But catching the ball was not his only talent. Once the ball was in his hands, Lamb often found the end zone.

In a 2019 highlight-reel moment, the score was tied 10–10 against Texas. Oklahoma quarterback Jalen Hurts passed to Lamb. Texas defenders were everywhere. But Lamb got by them. He sprinted 51 yards to the end zone for a touchdown. He had 10 receptions and three total touchdowns in that game. Oklahoma beat Texas 34–27.

Lamb leaps to make a catch in a game for Oklahoma.

Lamb played with some of college football's best quarterbacks at Oklahoma. Two were Heisman Trophy winners. With all that talent, the Oklahoma Sooners were a football powerhouse. They were champions of the Big 12 Conference for all three seasons Lamb played.

Over Lamb's three years as a Sooner, he made 173 receptions. He also had 3,292 receiving yards. He scored 32 touchdowns. In 2019, he was a runner-up for

SUPER SPORTS SCOOP

One of Lamb's most amazing catches at Oklahoma did not count. He leaped about 3 feet (0.9 m) in the air and grabbed the ball with one hand. He then somersaulted to the ground. But he landed out of bounds. The pass was incomplete.

Lamb (*left*) reaches for a pass at the Sooners' stadium in 2018.

the Biletnikoff Award. It is given each year to college football's best wide receiver.

After three years of college football, players can choose to enter the NFL draft. At the annual draft, NFL teams take turns picking new players. In late 2019, Lamb decided to be in the 2020 draft. He was headed to the pros.

CHAPTER 3

AMERICA'S TEAM

In the 2020 NFL draft, the Dallas Cowboys chose CeeDee Lamb as the 17th overall pick. Lamb signed a four-year contract worth about $14 million. He moved to Dallas, Texas. Lamb played well in his first season. He had 74 receptions, 935 receiving yards, and five touchdowns.

Despite this, the Cowboys had a losing record. They had six wins and 10 losses.

Lamb took his catching ability to the Dallas Cowboys in 2020.

SUPER SPORTS SCOOP

CeeDee Lamb is the newest member of Club 88. The club includes great Dallas receivers who have worn the number 88 on their jerseys. The other famous members are Drew Pearson, Michael Irvin, and Dez Bryant.

But 2021 was a different story. The Cowboys came out blazing. They won four of their first five games. The Dallas offense had many skilled receivers. But quarterback Dak Prescott often chose to throw to Lamb. Lamb could slip past his defenders, snag passes, and find the end zone.

On October 17, 2021, Lamb caught six passes in regulation time against the New England Patriots.

The game went into overtime tied 29–29. The Patriots were forced to punt. Prescott led the Cowboys into Patriots territory. Along the way, he hit Lamb with two more key receptions.

Finally, Prescott threw the ball 35 yards to Lamb. Lamb was open near the end zone. He made the catch and ran in for the winning touchdown.

Lamb catches a pass for the win against the New England Patriots on October 17, 2021.

Lamb ended the 2021 season with 79 receptions. He also had 1,102 receiving yards and six touchdowns. The Cowboys won 12 games and lost five. They earned a spot in the playoffs. This series of games leads up to the Super Bowl. In the first round of the playoffs, the Cowboys lost to the San Francisco 49ers. The season was over for the Cowboys.

Lamb (*right*) moves swiftly on the field in a 2021 game against the New Orleans Saints.

Lamb scores a touchdown at the NFL Pro Bowl Games in 2024.

The next season, Dallas again went 12–5. But this time, they lost in the second round of the playoffs. Lamb, however, kept getting better. He had 107 receptions, 1,359 receiving yards, and nine touchdowns in 2022. Sportswriter Jerry Trotta knew Lamb was getting better every season. "Lamb is about to be unstoppable," Trotta said.

CHAPTER 4

UNSTOPPABLE

Lamb kept getting better in the 2023 season. He set Cowboys single-season records for receptions and receiving yards. He also led the entire NFL with 135 receptions. His 1,749 receiving yards were the second most in the league.

The Cowboys again made the playoffs after another season of 12 wins and five losses. In the first round, they were expected to beat the Green Bay Packers. The Packers had a 9–8 record. But the Packers played like champions that day. They beat the Cowboys 48–32.

Lamb dodges Packers players for a touchdown in 2022.

Lamb and his teammates were disappointed. After the game, Lamb said that attitude is a big part of winning or losing. He promised to be a leader in the future. He wants to inspire his teammates with positive energy.

Lamb has fame and fortune as a football star. His sponsors include Nike, Pizza Hut, and Lowe's. He enjoys time off the field with his dogs, Saint and Hendrix. He also likes to help at local charities and community groups.

SUPER SPORTS SCOOP

At its yearly NFL Honors ceremony, the league names the most valuable player and hands out other awards. For the 2023 season, the NFL honored CeeDee Lamb and his 92-yard touchdown catch. The catch was named the 2023 NFL Moment of the Year.

Lamb takes in the packed stadium before the Cowboys faced the Packers in a playoff game in January 2024.

One of these is the Elephant in the Room, which helps people dealing with mental health challenges. He also supports the Boys & Girls Clubs of Greater Dallas.

Lamb runs toward the end zone in a 2023 game against the Seattle Seahawks.

Lamb has his eye on the biggest prize in football: a Super Bowl victory. “A successful year is winning the Super Bowl,” he said in 2023. “I want a [championship] ring.” With his talent and drive on the football field, that ring may be in CeeDee Lamb’s future.

Lamb makes a catch in a game against the Lions on December 30, 2023.

CEEDEE LAMB CAREER STATS

PRO GAMES PLAYED:

66

RECEPTIONS:

395

RECEIVING YARDS:

5,145

TOUCHDOWNS:

32

GLOSSARY

conference: one of several parts of a sports league. Teams in a conference play most of their games against one another.

end zone: the areas at each end of a football field where players score touchdowns

Heisman Trophy: a yearly award given to the best college football player

overtime: an extra period of play to determine the winner if a football game is tied after regulation time

receiving yards: the number of yards gained on a passing play. The total includes the length of the pass and the additional yards gained by running.

reception: a completed pass

regulation time: the normal length of a football game

scholarship: money to help pay for someone's education

sponsor: a business that pays a person to appear in advertisements and to promote products

SOURCE NOTES

6 Patrik Walker, "CeeDee Lamb Passes Irvin, Owns Cowboys' Records," Dallas Cowboys, December 31, 2023, https://www.dallascowboys.com/news/ceedee-lamb-passes-irvin-owns-cowboys-records.

11 Pat Doney, "CeeDee Lamb's Journey to the Dallas Cowboys," NBCDFW, April 24, 2020, https://nbcdfw.com/news/sports/ceedee-lambs-journey-to-the-dallas cowboys/2357879.

21 Jerry Trotta, "Cowboys' CeeDee Lamb About to Become Unstoppable with Workout Request," the Landry Hat, April 7, 2023, https://thelandryhat.com/2023/04/07/cowboys-ceedee-lamb-become-unstoppable-workout-request-video.

27 Adam Schultz, "CeeDee Lamb Reveals Cowboys Season Goal: 'I Want a Ring,'" Dallas Cowboys on SI, August 6, 2023, https://www.si.com/nfl/cowboys/news/dallas-cowboys-season-goal-ceedee-lamb-super-bowl-ring-offense-brandin-cooks-training-camp.

LEARN MORE

Anderson, Josh. *G.O.A.T. Football Wide Receivers.* Minneapolis: Lerner Publications, 2024.

Dallas Cowboys Facts
https://www.softschools.com/facts/sports/dallas_cowboys_facts/1363/

Football: National Football League
https://www.ducksters.com/sports/national_football_league.php

Hill, Christina. *Inside the Dallas Cowboys.* Minneapolis: Lerner Publications, 2023.

Kiddle: National Football League Facts for Kids
https://kids.kiddle.co/National_Football_League

Lynne, Douglas. *Dak Prescott: NFL Star.* Burnsville, MN: Press Room Editions, 2024.

INDEX

PHOTO ACKNOWLEDGMENTS

Image credits: AP Photo/James D. Smith, pp. 4, 17; AP Photo/Michael Ainsworth, p. 6; Perry Knotts/Getty Images, p. 7; Stephen M. Dowell/Orlando Sentinel/Tribune News Service/Getty Images, p. 8; joeynick/Getty Images, p. 9; James Nielsen/Houston Chronicle/Getty Images, p. 11; Chad Robertson Media/Shutterstock, p. 12; Richard Rowe/Icon Sportswire/Getty Images, p. 13; Tom Pennington/Getty Images, p. 15; AP Photo/Ron Jenkins, p. 16; Maddie Meyer/Getty Images, p. 19; AP Photo/Aaron M. Sprecher, p. 20; Megan Briggs/Getty Images, p. 21; Michael Owens/Getty Images, p. 22; AP Photo/Matt Ludtke, p. 23; Cooper Neill/Getty Images, p. 25; AP Photo/Michael Owens, p. 26; AP Photo/Perry Knotts, p. 27.

Cover: AP Photo/Tom DiPace.